THE DISCOVER CATS
EXPLORE ANCIENT EGYPT

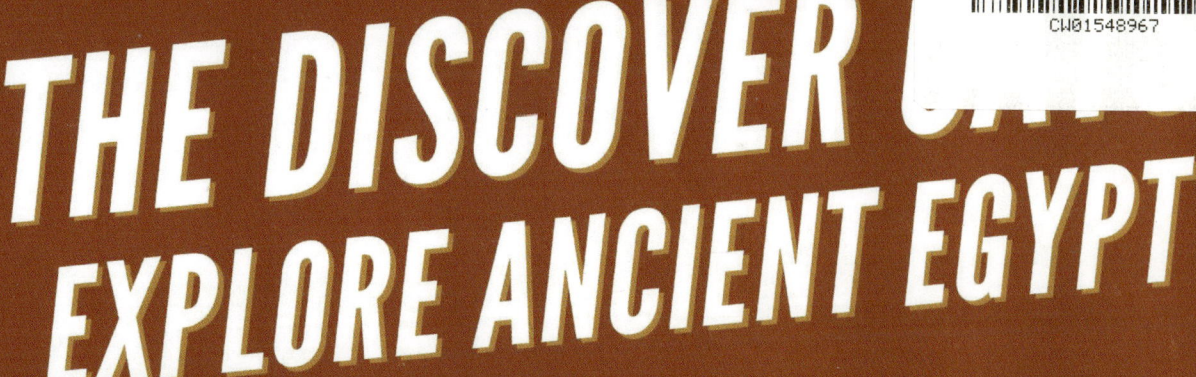

WRITTEN BY JIMMY NIGHTINGALE & ILLUSTRATED BY GRACE JI

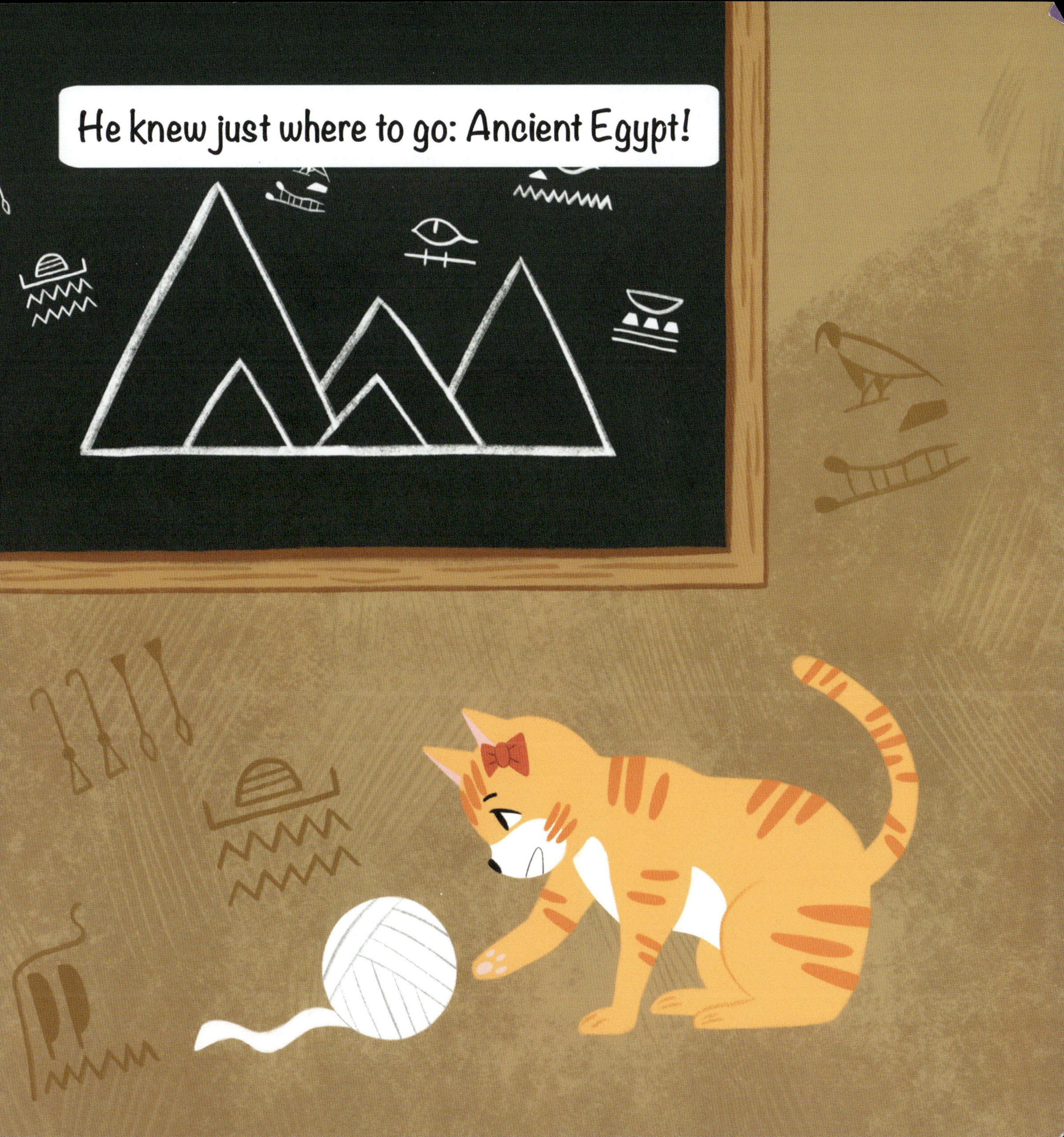
He knew just where to go: Ancient Egypt!

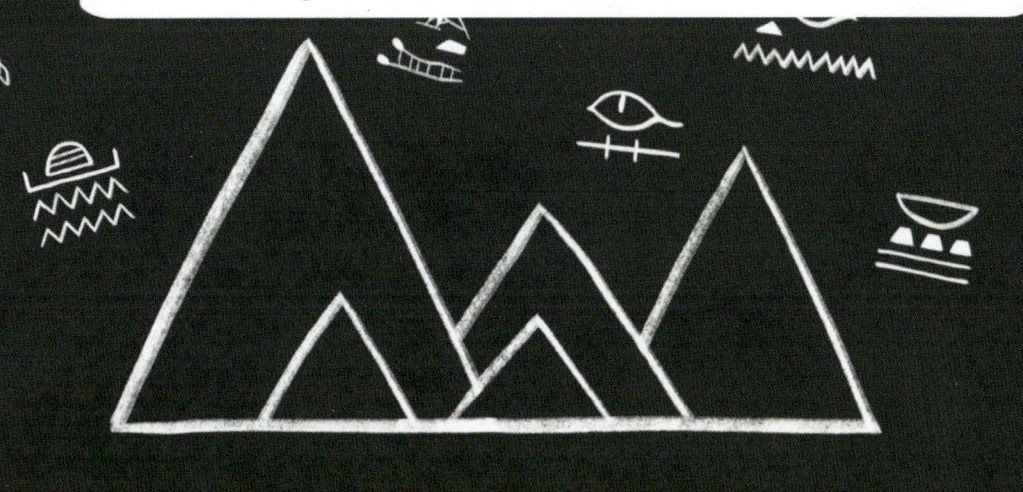

Cornelius developed a top-secret time travel machine.

He called Max and Ginny in, closed the hatch, and off they went.

Cornelius started explaining, "You've probably heard of mummies, pyramids, hieroglyphics, and Pharaohs. They all come from Ancient Egypt!"

"Pharaohs loved to build pyramids so people would remember them. Pyramids were used as tombs, and they used to be beautiful and shiny on the outside. Pharaohs were also buried with lots of their treasure."

Cornelius said, "The Egyptians loved to build big structures to honor these gods, for example Abu Simbel, the Sphinx, and Luxor."

Cornelius said, "They were also amazing at early medicine and astronomy."

Printed in Great Britain
by Amazon